NEUROANATOMY
AND
NEUROTRANSMITTERS

ACADEMIC COLORING BOOK AND STUDY GUIDE

CHRISTINA MAROONE

ILLUSTRATED BY ADDISON COOPER

Neuroanatomy And Neurotransmitters: Academic Coloring Book and Study Guide

Copyright 2023 Christina Maroone

For questions, comments, and updates, please visit www.AcademicColoringBooks.com or email info@academiccoloringbooks.com

About the Author

Christina Maroone is a board-certified psychiatric mental health nurse practitioner (PMHNP) specializing in medication management and psychotherapy. She practices in New York City where she lives with her husband and two children. She is completing her Doctor of Nursing Practice at Yale University with a focus in Healthcare Leadership, Systems, and Policy. She holds a Post-Master's PMHNP Certificate from New York University, a Master of Science in Nursing Administration from Hunter-Bellevue School of Nursing, a Master of Public Administration from Baruch College, and a Bachelor of Science in Nursing from Russell Sage College.

In her previous roles, Christina served as a patient care director for inpatient psychiatry at New York Presbyterian Hospital (Columbia) and managed the emergency department at New York Presbyterian Hospital (Cornell). She continues to teach as an adjunct clinical professor at New York University and holds a board-member-at-large position on the American Psychiatric Nurses Association's New York Chapter.

Christina is passionate about creating fun and accessible ways to learn. As an undergraduate nursing student, her anatomy and physiology professor regularly assigned coloring pages to help students memorize anatomy. The ability to learn kinesthetically through coloring was unique and stimulating, yet simple. This left a lasting impression on Christina and eventually led her to create this coloring book to share with others to facilitate the learning process.

Introduction
Coloring Promotes Memorization

This coloring book provides a supplemental learning resource to anyone interested in learning about neuroanatomy and neurotransmitters. Key information is provided with corresponding illustrations on these topics. Students are able to visualize and memorize both basic and complex processes through hands-on learning. When a student slows down to read and color the text and illustrations in this book, visual associations between key neuroanatomical structures and neurotransmitters are made. This non-traditional way of learning will help students with understanding and retaining information about neuroanatomy and neurotransmitters.

It is recommended that you follow the coloring strategies below to give structure to the coloring book and augment the learning process. Be sure to color the words on each page, as this will help promote memorization.

This book is divided into two parts: Part 1 Neuroanatomy and Part 2 Neurotransmitters.

Part One: Neuroanatomy

Nervous System: Color the parasympathetic nerves with one color and the sympathetic nerves with a second color.

Lobes of the Brain: Color each lobe of the brain and its corresponding responsibilities with the same color.

Anatomy of the Brain: Color each numbered area of the brain and its corresponding name with the same color.

Part Two: Neurotransmitters

Parts of a Neuron: Color each numbered area of the neuron and its corresponding name with the same color.

Neurotransmitters: Choose two colors for each neurotransmitter. Use one color for the "too little" column and the second color for the "too much" column. You can use these two colors freely throughout the rest of the neurotransmitter description and illustrations.

COLORED PENCILS ARE RECOMMENDED.
HAPPY COLORING!

Table of Contents

PART ONE - NEUROANATOMY

Nervous System 2

Autonomic Nervous System 3

Frontal Lobe 4

Parietal Lobe 5

Occipital Lobe 6

Temporal Lobe 7

Cerebellum 8

Pons 9

Medulla Oblongata 10

Insula 11

Anatomy of the Brain: Sagittal View 12

Functional Areas of the Brain: Lateral View 14

Limbic System: Sagittal View 16

Thalamus 18

Coronal Section of the Brain 20

Cranial Nerves: Inferior View 22

The Circle of Willis 24

Protective Structures of the Brain 26

PART TWO - NEUROTRANSMITTERS

Parts of a Neuron 30

Synapse 32

Neurochemistry 33

Serotonin 34

Dopamine 36

Norepinephrine 38

Acetylcholine 40

Gaba 42

Glutamate 44

Endorphins 46

Histamine 48

PART ONE
NEUROANATOMY

NERVOUS SYSTEM

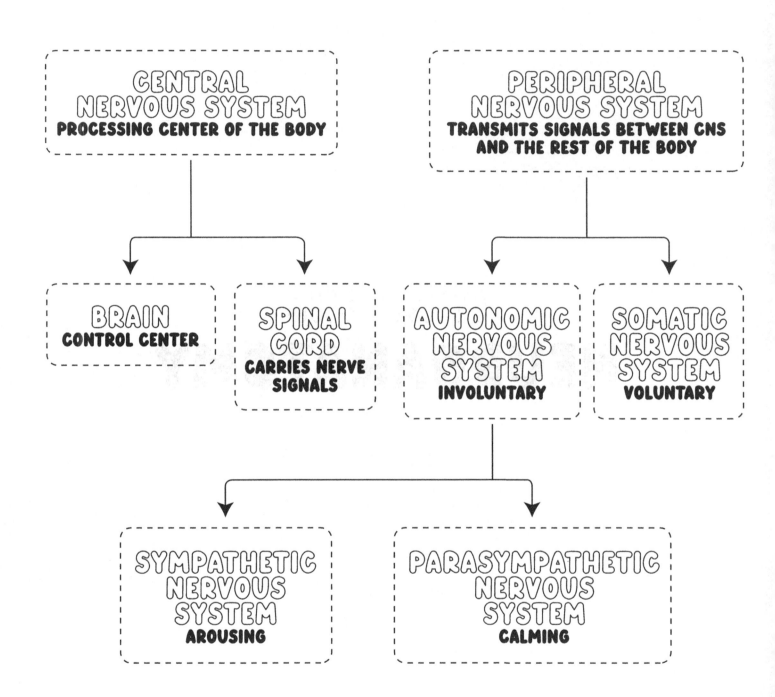

CENTRAL
NERVOUS SYSTEM
PROCESSING CENTER OF THE BODY

PERIPHERAL
NERVOUS SYSTEM
**TRANSMITS SIGNALS BETWEEN CNS
AND THE REST OF THE BODY**

BRAIN
CONTROL CENTER

SPINAL
CORD
**CARRIES NERVE
SIGNALS**

AUTONOMIC
NERVOUS
SYSTEM
INVOLUNTARY

SOMATIC
NERVOUS
SYSTEM
VOLUNTARY

SYMPATHETIC
NERVOUS
SYSTEM
AROUSING

PARASYMPATHETIC
NERVOUS
SYSTEM
CALMING

AUTONOMIC NERVOUS SYSTEM

PARASYMPATHETIC NERVES

 CONSTRICT PUPILS

 STIMULATE SALIVA

 CONSTRICT AIRWAYS

 DECREASE HEART RATE

 INHIBIT RELEASE OF GLUCOSE

 STIMULATE GALLBLADDER

 STIMULATE GI ACTIVITY

 CONTRACT BLADDER

 PROMOTE ERECTION OF GENITALS

CENTRAL NERVOUS SYSTEM

PERIPHERAL NERVOUS SYSTEM

SYMPATHETIC NERVES

DILATE PUPILS

INHIBIT SALIVATION

RELAX AIRWAYS

INCREASE HEART RATE

STIMULATE RELEASE OF GLUCOSE

INHIBIT GALLBLADDER

INHIBIT GI ACTIVITY

SECRETE EPINEPHRINE AND NOREPINEPHRINE

RELAX BLADDER

PROMOTE EJACULATION/ VAGINAL CONTRACTIONS

FRONTAL LOBE

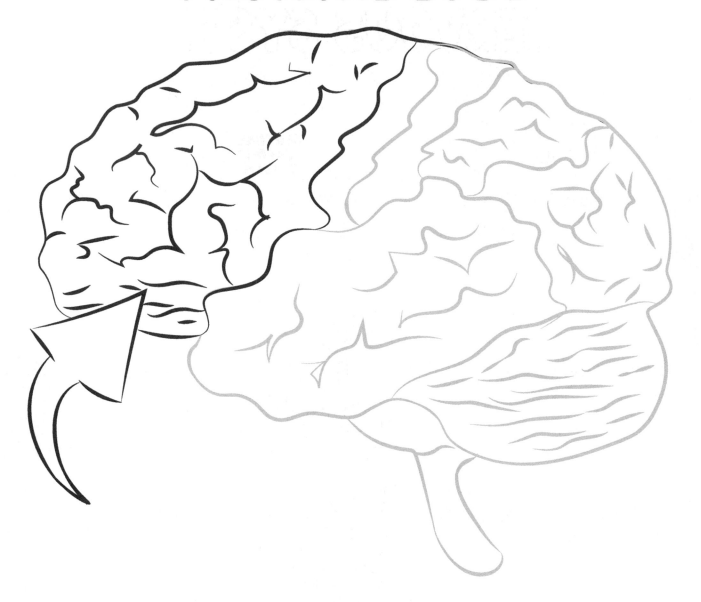

RESPONSIBLE FOR:

BEHAVIOR

PLANNING

REASONING

MOTOR MOVEMENT

PROBLEM SOLVING

PARIETAL LOBE

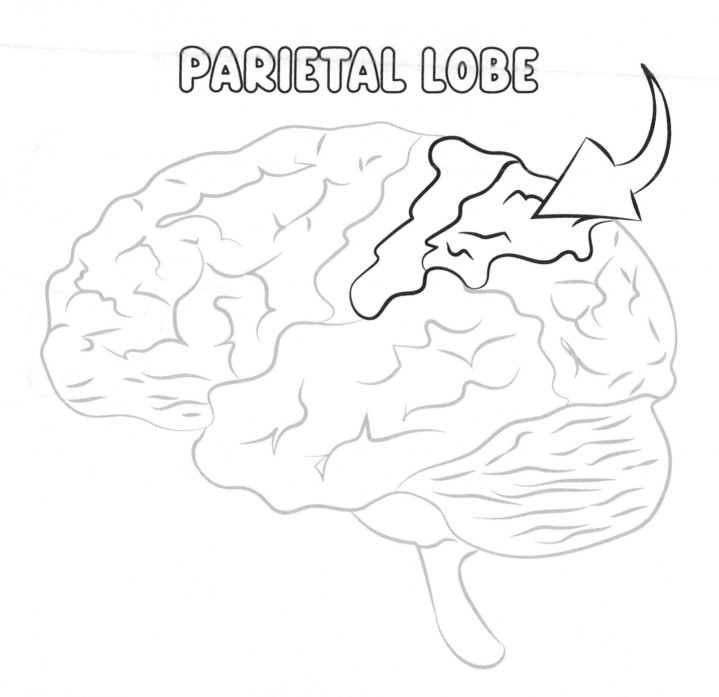

RESPONSIBLE FOR:

PROCESSING SENSORY INPUT
PROPRIOCEPTION

OCCIPITAL LOBE

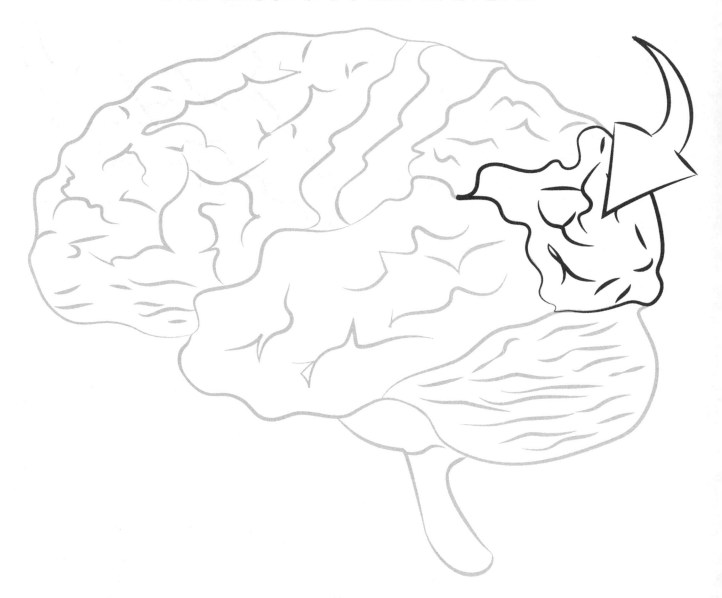

RESPONSIBLE FOR:

VISUAL PERCEPTION

TEMPORAL LOBE

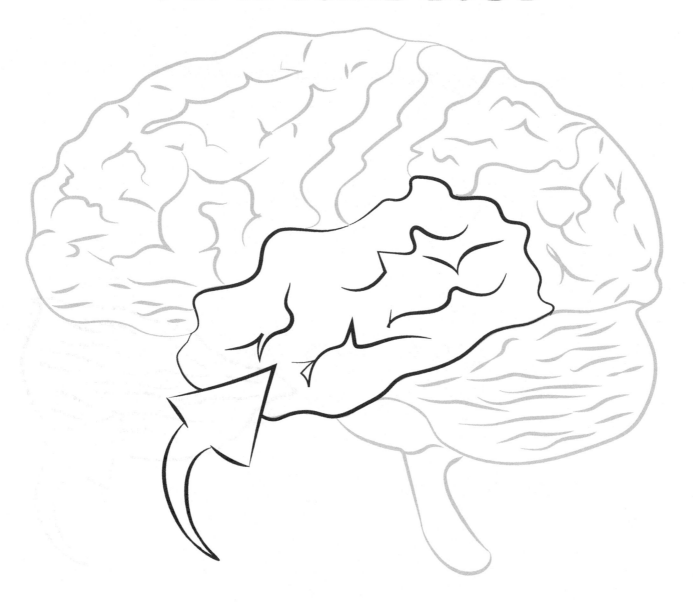

RESPONSIBLE FOR:

MEMORY

PROCESSING:

AFFECT

LANGUAGE

HEARING (LEFT SIDE)

CEREBELLUM

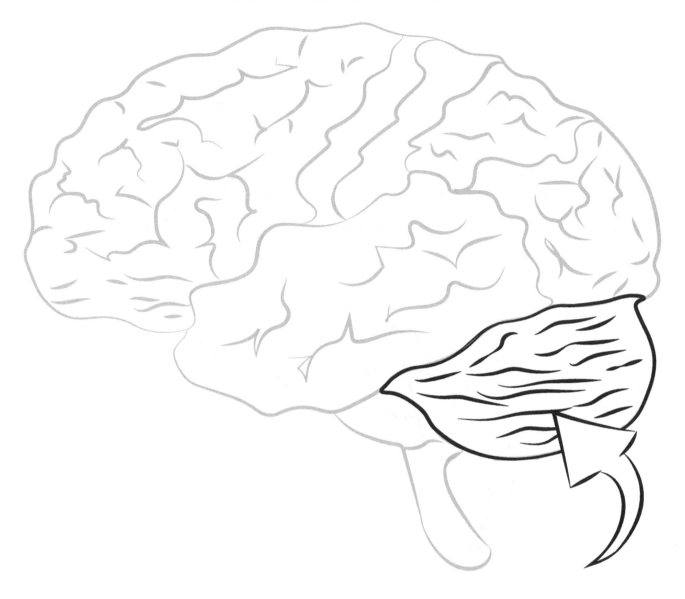

RESPONSIBLE FOR:

MOTOR SKILLS: POSTURE

COORDINATION   BALANCE

MOVEMENT   EQUILIBRIUM

COGNITIVE FUNCTION   SPEECH

PONS

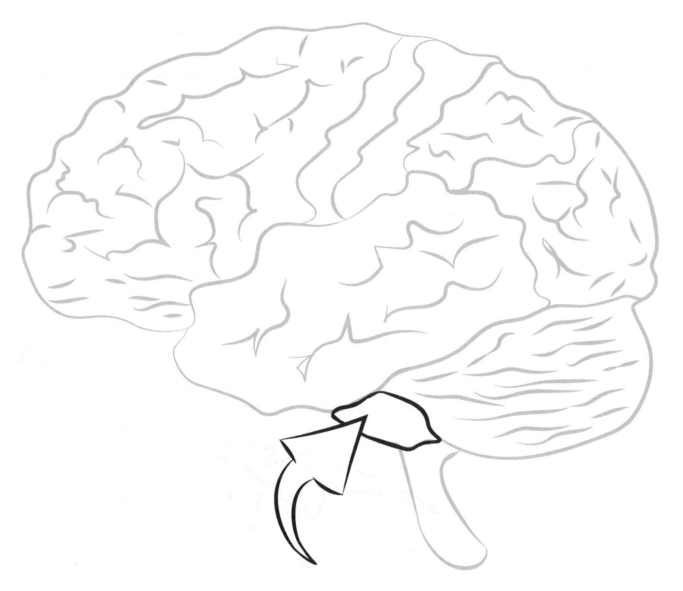

RESPONSIBLE FOR:

RELAYING INFORMATION BETWEEN CEREBRUM AND CEREBELLUM

RELAYING AND REGULATING PAIN SENSATIONS

RESPIRATION

SLEEP

MOTOR CONTROL

MEDULLA OBLONGATA

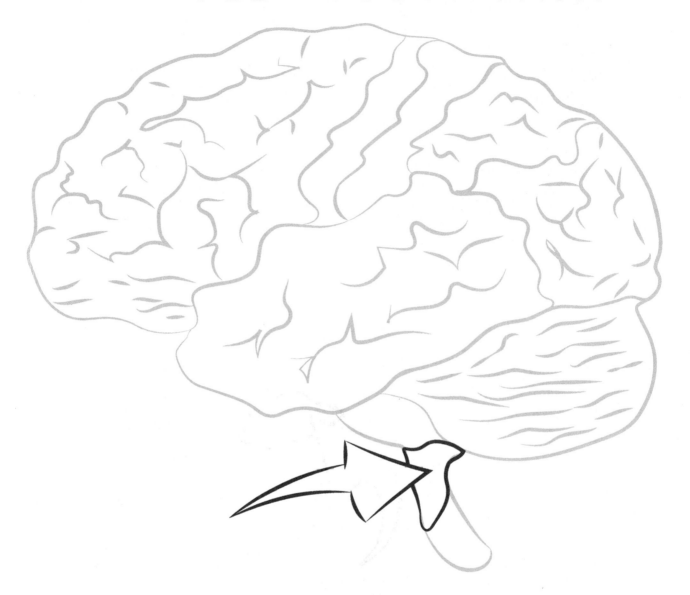

RESPONSIBLE FOR:

REGULATING INVOLUNTARY PROCESSES INCLUDING:

HORMONE RELEASE

RESPIRATION

HEART RATE

BLOOD PRESSURE

INSULA

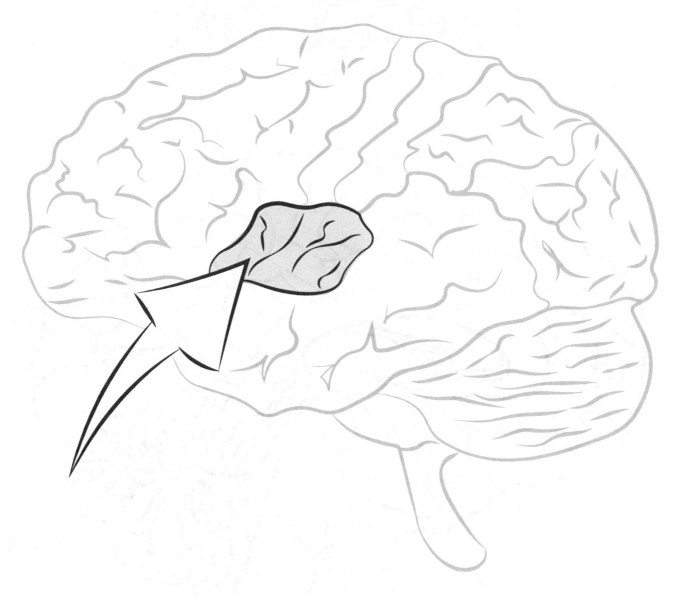

RESPONSIBLE FOR:

HOMEOSTATIC FUNCTIONS INCLUDING:

TASTE

VISCERAL SENSATION

AUTONOMIC CONTROL

ANATOMY OF THE BRAIN:
SAGITTAL VIEW

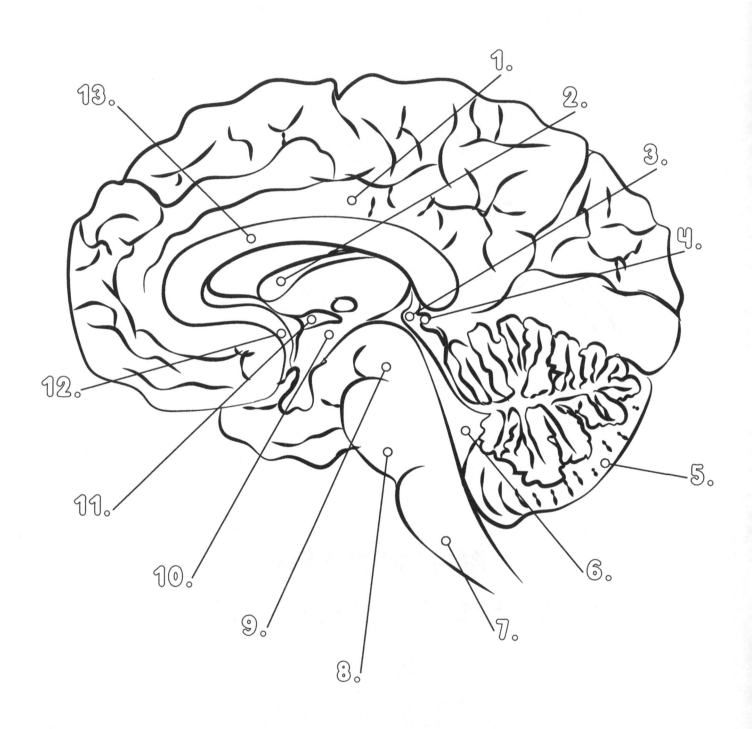

ANATOMY OF THE BRAIN:
SAGITTAL VIEW

1. CINGULATE GYRUS

2. FORNIX

3. PINEAL GLAND

4. POSTERIOR COMMISSURE

5. CEREBELLUM

6. FOURTH VENTRICLE

7. MEDULLA OBLONGATA

8. PONS

9. MIDBRAIN

10. HYPOTHALAMIC SULCUS

11. DIENCEPHALON

12. ANTERIOR COMMISSURE

13. CORPUS CALLOSUM

FUNCTIONAL AREAS OF THE BRAIN:
LATERAL VIEW

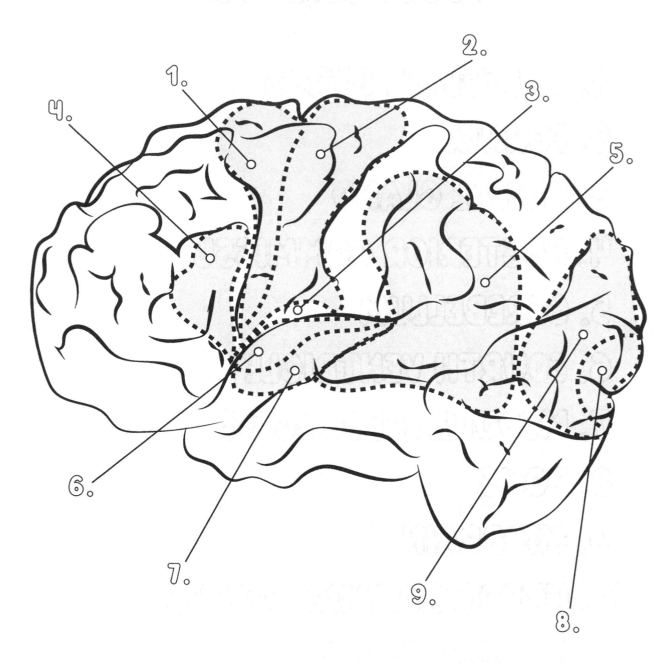

FUNCTIONAL AREAS OF THE BRAIN:
LATERAL VIEW

1. PRIMARY MOTOR AREA

2. PRIMARY SENSORY AREA

3. SECONDARY MOTOR AND SENSORY AREA

4. ANTERIOR (MOTOR) SPEECH AREA (BROCA'S AREA)

5. POSTERIOR (SENSORY) SPEECH AREA (WERNICKE'S AREA)

6. PRIMARY AUDITORY AREA

7. SECONDARY AUDITORY AREA

8. PRIMARY VISUAL AREA

9. SECONDARY VISUAL AREA

LIMBIC SYSTEM:
SAGITTAL VIEW

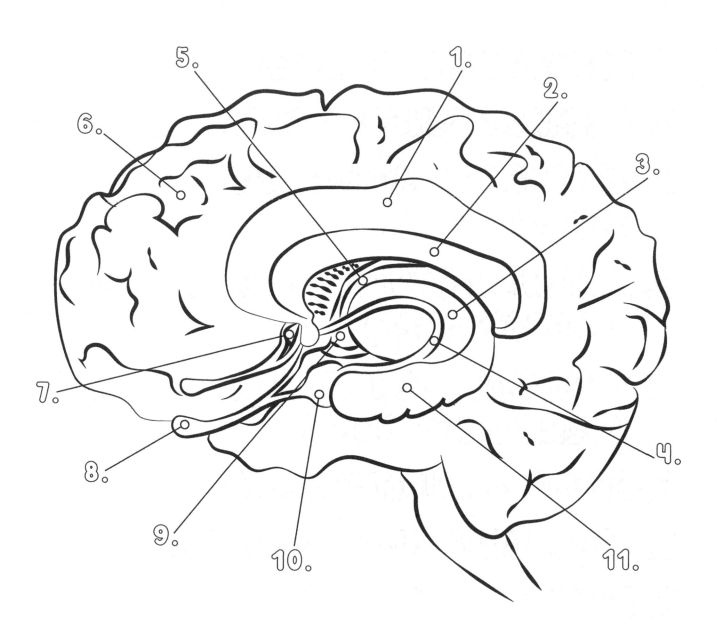

LIMBIC SYSTEM:
SAGITTAL VIEW

1. CINGULATE CORTEX
2. CORPUS CALLOSUM
3. THALAMUS
4. STRIA TERMINALIS
5. FORNIX
6. FRONTAL CORTEX
7. SEPTUM
8. OLFACTORY BULB
9. MAMMILLARY BODY
10. AMYGDALA
11. HIPPOCAMPUS

THALAMUS

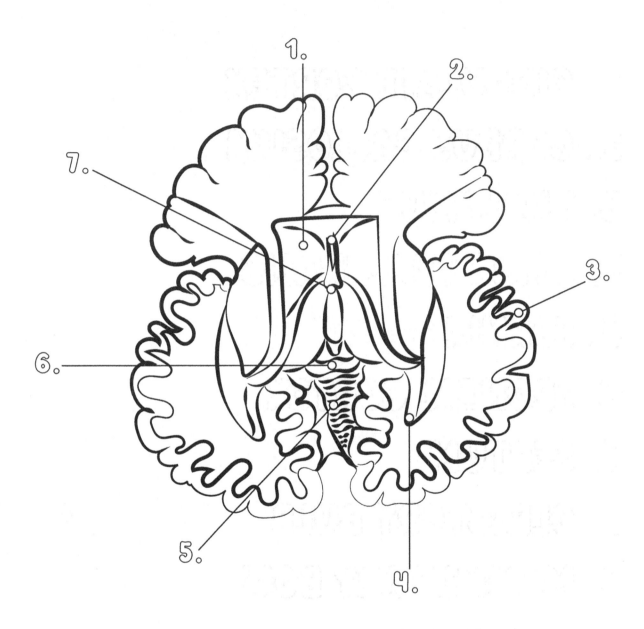

THALAMUS

1. HEAD OF CAUDATE NUCLEUS
2. CAVITY OF SEPTUM PELLUCIDUM
3. CORTEX OF TEMPORAL LOBE
4. POSTERIOR HORN OF LATERAL VENTRICLE
5. VERMIS OF CEREBELLUM
6. INFERIOR COILLCULUS
7. ANTERIOR COMMISSURE

CORONAL SECTION OF THE BRAIN

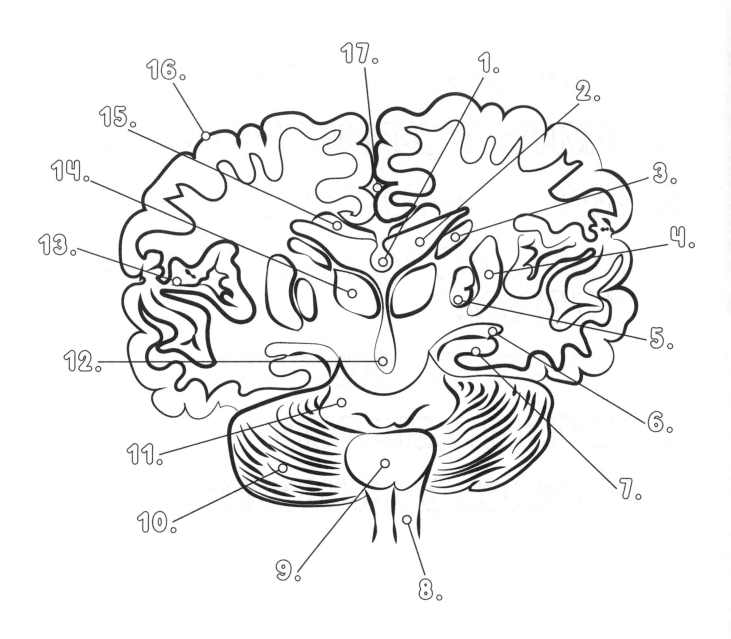

CORONAL SECTION OF THE BRAIN

1. FORNIX
2. LATERAL VENTRICLE
3. CAUDATE NUCLEUS
4. PUTAMEN
5. GLOBUS PALLIDUS
6. HIPPOCAMPUS
7. HIPPOCAMPAL GYRUS
8. SPINAL CORD
9. MEDULLA OBLONGATA
10. CEREBELLUM
11. PONS
12. THIRD VENTRICLE
13. LATERAL SULCUS
14. THALAMUS
15. CORPUS CALLOSUM
16. CEREBRAL CORTEX
17. LONGITUDINAL FISSURE

CRANIAL NERVES:
INFERIOR VIEW

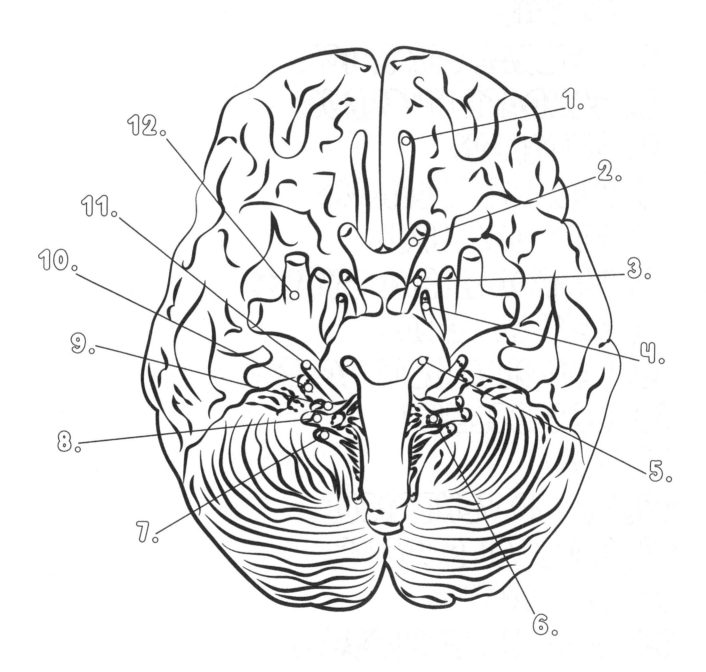

CRANIAL NERVES:
INFERIOR VIEW

1. OLFACTORY
2. OPTIC
3. OCULOMOTOR
4. TROCHLEAR
5. ABDUCENS
6. HYPOGLOSSAL
7. ACCESSORY
8. VAGUS
9. GLOSSOPHARYNGEAL
10. VESTIBULOCOCHLEAR
11. FACIAL
12. TRIGEMINAL

THE CIRCLE OF WILLIS

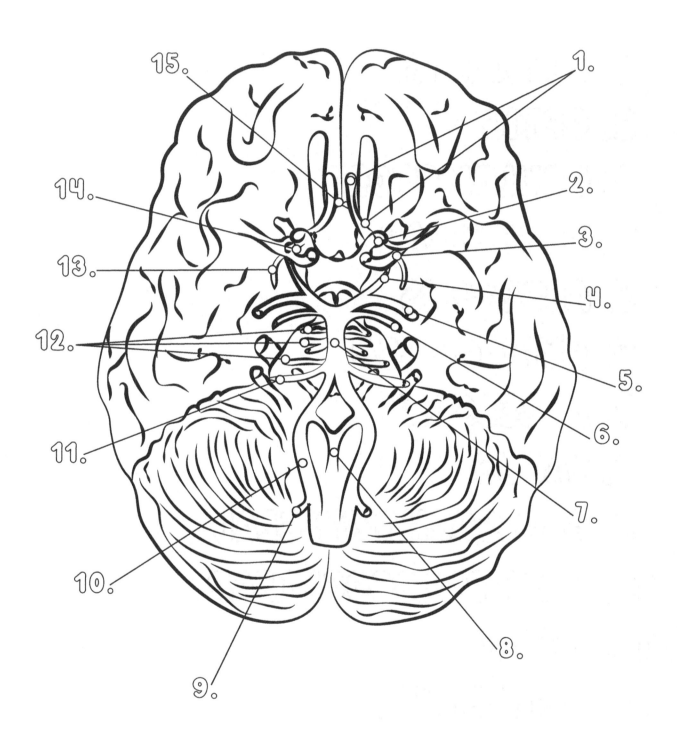

THE CIRCLE OF WILLIS

1. ANTERIOR CEREBRAL ARTERY
2. INTERAL CAROTID ARTERY
3. MIDDLE CEREBRAL ARTERY
4. POSTERIOR COMMUNICATING ARTERY
5. POSTERIOR CEREBRAL ARTERY
6. SUPERIOR CEREBELLAR ARTERY
7. BASILAR ARTERY
8. ANTERIOR SPINAL ARTERY
9. POSTERIOR INFERIOR CEREBELLAR ARTERY
10. VERTEBRAL ARTERY
11. ANTERIOR INFERIOR CEREBELLAR ARTERY
12. PONTINE ARTERIES
13. ANTERIOR CHOROIDAL ARTERY
14. OPHTALMIC ARTERY
15. ANTERIOR COMMUNICATING ARTERY

PROTECTIVE STRUCTURES OF THE BRAIN:

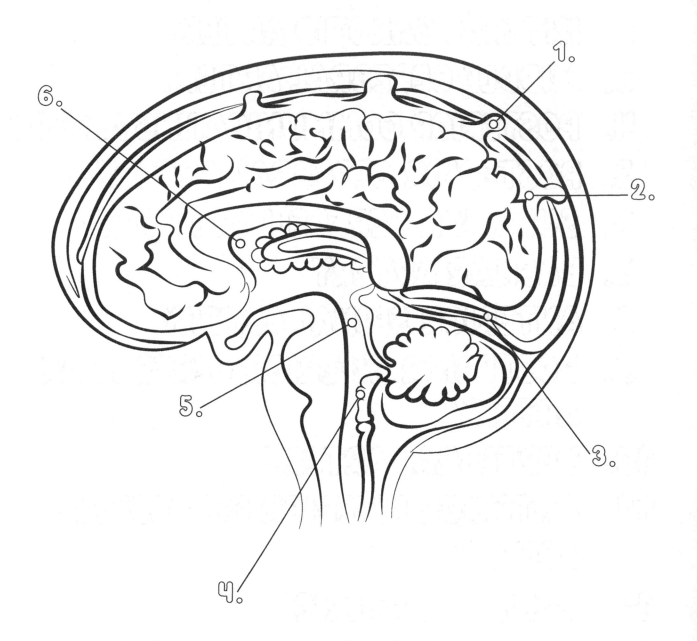

PROTECTIVE STRUCTURES OF THE BRAIN:

1. ARACHNOID VILLUS

2. SUBARACHNOID SPACE

3. STRAIGHT SINUS

4. CHOROID PLEXUS

5. CEREBRAL AQUEDUCT

6. THIRD VENTRICLE

PART TWO
NEUROTRANSMITTERS

PARTS OF A NEURON

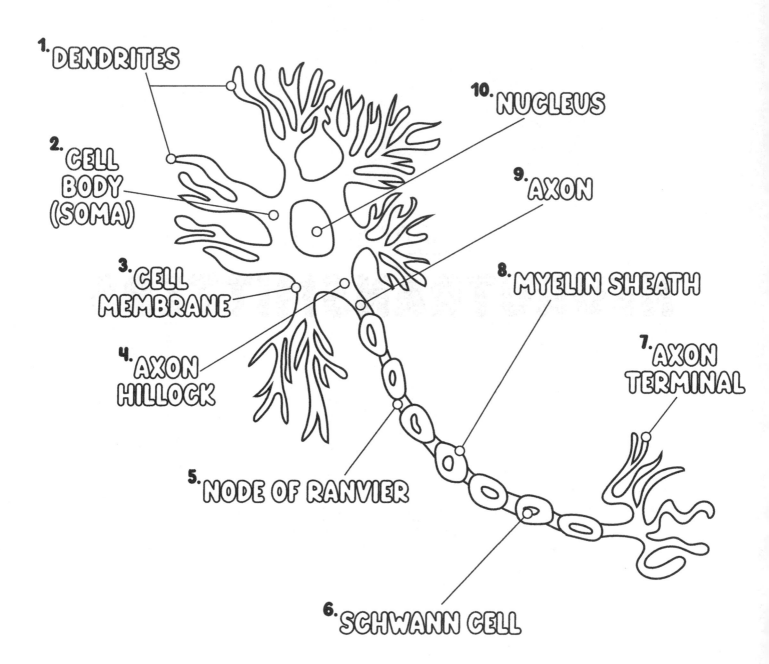

1. DENDRITES

2. CELL BODY (SOMA)

3. CELL MEMBRANE

4. AXON HILLOCK

5. NODE OF RANVIER

6. SCHWANN CELL

7. AXON TERMINAL

8. MYELIN SHEATH

9. AXON

10. NUCLEUS

PARTS OF A NEURON

1. RECEIVE IMPULSES FROM OTHER CELLS

2. HOUSES THE NUCLEUS

3. PROTECTS THE CELL

4. GENERATES IMPULSE DOWN THE AXON

5. FACILIATES RAPID CONDUCTION OF ELECTRICAL IMPLUSES ALONG THE AXON

6. PRODUCES THE MYELIN SHEATH AROUND AXONS

7. RELEASES NEUROTRANSMITTERS FROM THE PRESYNAPTIC CELL

8. INSULATOR THAT INCREASES THE SPEED OF ELECTRICAL IMPULSES

9. CARRIES IMPULSES AWAY FROM THE CELL BODY

10. CONTROLS THE NEURON

SYNAPSE

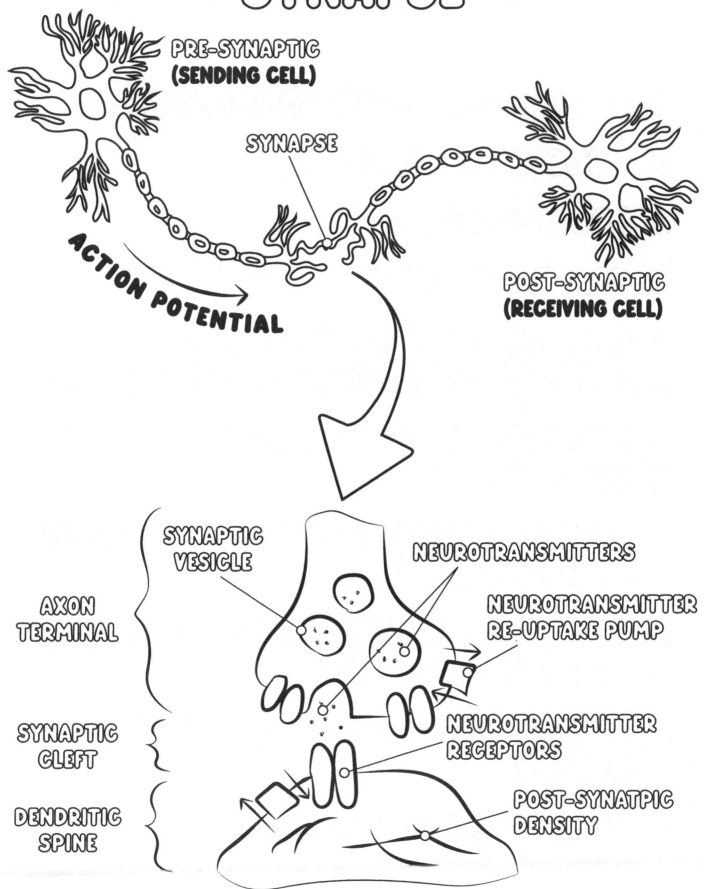

PRE-SYNAPTIC
(SENDING CELL)

SYNAPSE

POST-SYNAPTIC
(RECEIVING CELL)

ACTION POTENTIAL

SYNAPTIC
VESICLE

NEUROTRANSMITTERS

NEUROTRANSMITTER
RE-UPTAKE PUMP

AXON
TERMINAL

NEUROTRANSMITTER
RECEPTORS

SYNAPTIC
CLEFT

DENDRITIC
SPINE

POST-SYNATPIC
DENSITY

NEUROCHEMISTRY

Monoamine neurotransmitter systems modulate a variety of neuronal pathways, which impact multiple behavioral and psychological processes. There are a number of these neurotransmitters presented in this text, which are critical to psychopharmacology. These chemical neurotransmitters transmit signals across the synapse between neurotransmitters. These neurotransmitters are the targets of psychotropic medications.

CLASSIFICATION OF KEY NEUROTRANSMITTERS

Biogenic amines (monoamines / bioamines)

- DOPAMINE
- NOREPINEPHRINE (NORADRENALIN)
- EPINEPHRINE (ADRENALINE)
- SEROTONIN
- HISTAMINE

Cholinergics

- ACETYLCHOLINE

Amino acids

- GLUTAMATE
- GABA
- GLYCINE

Neuropeptides

- OPIOID & NONOPIOID NEUROPEPTIDES

Neurotransmitters can be described as excitatory, inhibitory, or both. Excitatory neurotransmitters increase the likelihood of cell firing while inhibitory neurotransmitters decrease the likelihood of cell firing for example:

Excitatory

- INCREASE LIKELIHOOD OF CELL FIRING
- EX: GLUTAMATE, NOREPINEPHRINE (NE)

Inhibitory

- DECREASE LIKELIHOOD OF CELL FIRING
- EX: GABA, SEROTONIN (5HT)

Mixed

- CAN HAVE EXCITATORY OR INHIBITORY EFFECTS
- EX: ACETYLCHOLINE (ACH), DOPAMINE (DA)

33

NEUROTRANSMITTER:
SEROTONIN

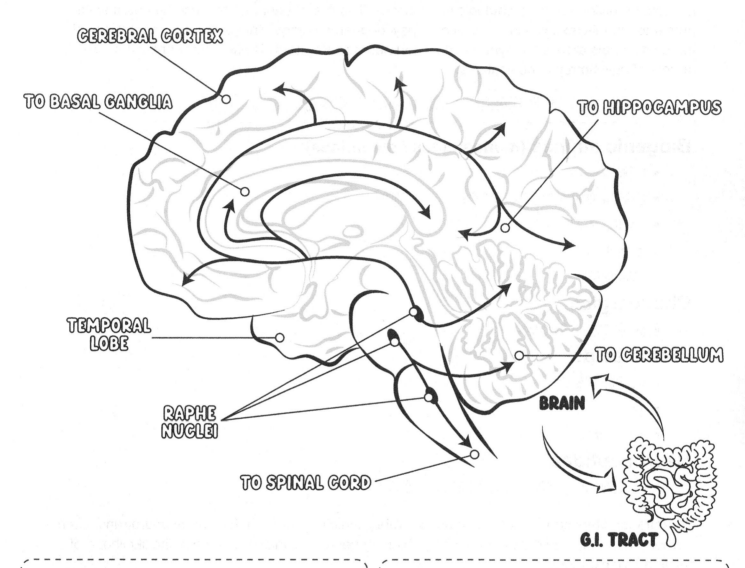

CEREBRAL CORTEX

TO BASAL GANGLIA

TO HIPPOCAMPUS

TEMPORAL LOBE

TO CEREBELLUM

RAPHE NUCLEI

BRAIN

TO SPINAL CORD

G.I. TRACT

PRODUCED IN:
RAPHE NUCLEI

PATHWAYS:
DISTRIBUTION OF SEROTONIN FROM RAPHE NUCLEI THROUGH THE CORTEX AND INTO THE CEREBELLUM

MAJOR FUNCTIONS OF NEUROTRANSMITTER:
MOOD REGULATION
HUNGER
SLEEP-WAKE CYCLE
SEXUAL DESIRE
COGNITION
SENSORY PERCEPTIONS
G.I. MOTILITY

NEUROTRANSMITTER:
SEROTONIN

TOO LITTLE...

POOR MEMORY

POOR APPETITE

ANXIETY

IRRITABILITY

LOW SELF-ESTEEM

INSOMNIA

DEPRESSION

TOO MUCH...

MILD:

SHIVERING, DIARRHEA,

HYPERACTIVITY, PUPIL DILATION

SEVERE (SEROTONIN SYNDROME):

MUSCLE RIGIDITY, FEVER,

RHABDOMYOLYSIS,

SEIZURES, DEATH

NEUROTRANSMITTER:
DOPAMINE

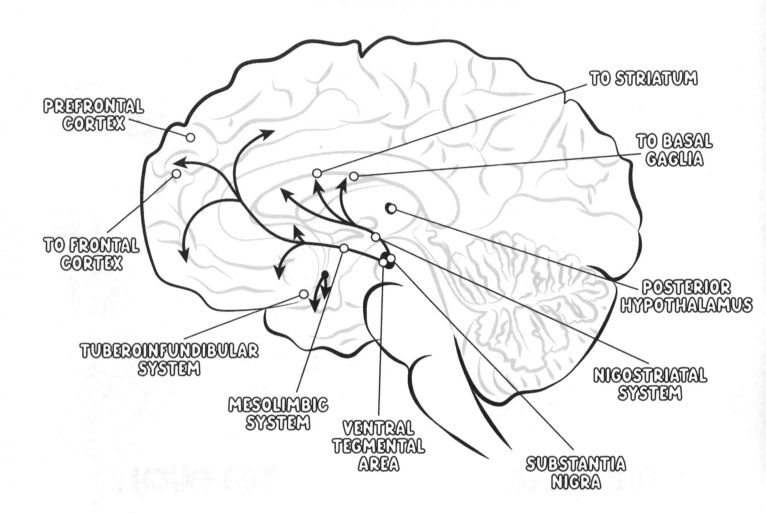

PRODUCED IN:
VENTRAL TEGMENTAL AREA (VTA),
SUBSTANTIA NIGRA, ARCUATE
NUCLEUS OF THE HYPOTHALAMUS

PATHWAYS:
MESOLIMBIC, TUBEROINFUNDIBULAR,
MESOCORTICAL, NIGROSTRIATAL

MAJOR FUNCTIONS OF NEUROTRANSMITTER:
MOTOR MOVEMENT
ALERTNESS / ATTENTION
AGGRESSION
THINKING
PLANNING
COGNITION
PLEASURE AND PAIN
MOOD REGULATION

NEUROTRANSMITTER:
DOPAMINE

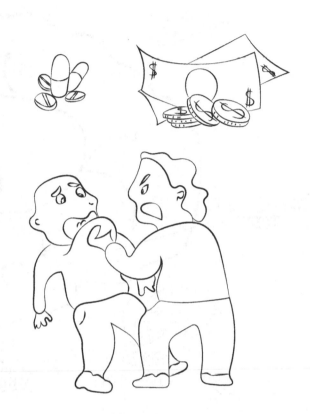

TOO LITTLE...

REDUCED ALERTNESS,
DIFFICULTY CONCENTRATING,
LACK OF MOTIVATION,
POOR COORDINATION,
MOVEMENT DIFFICULTIES,
INABILITY TO FEEL PLEASURE,
RESTLESS LEGS,
PARKINSON'S DISEASE

TOO MUCH...

EUPHORIA, HALLUCINATIONS,
DELUSIONS, AGGRESSION, ADDICTION,
COMPETITIVE BEHAVIORS,
POOR IMPULSE CONTROL,
GAMBLING BEHAVIORS,
MANIA, PSYCHOSIS

NEUROTRANSMITTER:
NOREPINEPHRINE

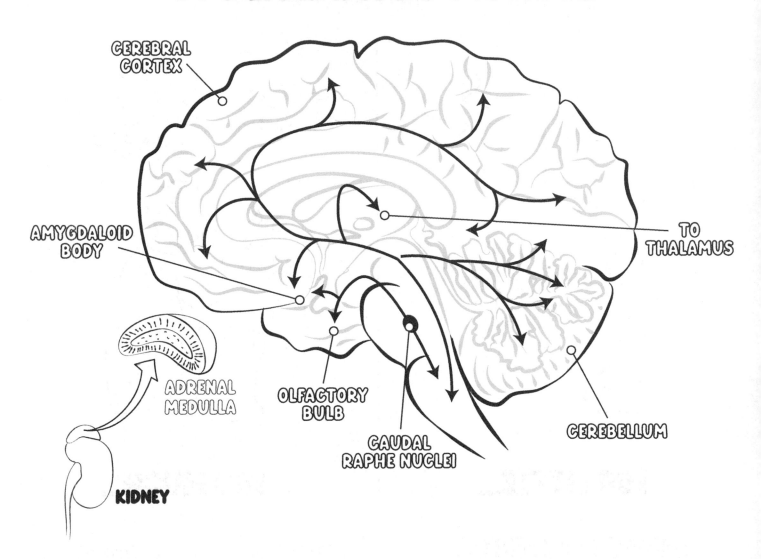

CEREBRAL CORTEX

AMYGDALOID BODY

ADRENAL MEDULLA

KIDNEY

OLFACTORY BULB

CAUDAL RAPHE NUCLEI

TO THALAMUS

CEREBELLUM

PRODUCED IN:
LOCUS COERULEUS OF BRAINSTEM AND ADRENAL MEDULLA OF ADRENAL GLANDS

PATHWAYS:
CNS: COMES FROM THE LOCUS COERULEUS
PNS: COMES FROM ADRENAL MEDULLA

MAJOR FUNCTIONS OF NEUROTRANSMITTER:
FIGHT OR FLIGHT, ALERTNESS, AROUSAL, MOOD, EATING, ATTENTION, MEMORY, LEARNING, SLEEP

INCREASES:
HEART RATE
BLOOD PRESSURE
RESPIRATIONS

NEUROTRANSMITTER:
NOREPINEPHRINE

TOO LITTLE...

DIFFICULTY FOCUSING
HEADACHES
MEMORY PROBLEMS
SLEEPING PROBLEMS
LOW ENERGY
HYPOTENSION
DEPRESSION
ADHD

TOO MUCH...

HYPERTENSION,

RAPID OR IRREGULAR HEARTBEAT,

INCREASED RESPIRATORY RATE,

INCREASED ENERGY/MOVEMENT,

EXCESSIVE SWEATING, COLD OR PALE SKIN,

SEVERE HEADACHES, JITTERS, SHAKING,

ANXIETY, MANIA

NEUROTRANSMITTER:
ACETYLCHOLINE

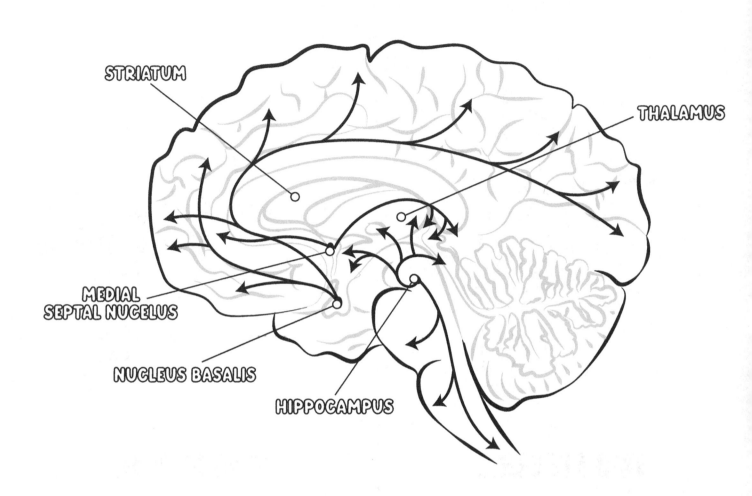

STRIATUM

THALAMUS

MEDIAL
SEPTAL NUCELUS

NUCLEUS BASALIS

HIPPOCAMPUS

PRODUCED IN:
BASAL FOREBRAIN

PATHWAYS:
LATERAL TEGMENTAL AREA TO THE STRIATAL
REGEIONS OF THE BASAL GANGLIA

MAJOR FUNCTIONS OF NEUROTRANSMITTER:

AROUSAL

MOTOR MOVEMENT

LEARNING AND MEMORY

REM (DREAM) SLEEP

NEUROTRANSMITTER:
ACETYLCHOLINE

TOO LITTLE...

IMPAIRED MEMORY

MOOD SWINGS

BIPOLAR DISORDER

DEPRESSION

ALZHEIMER'S DISEASE

TOO MUCH...

ANXIETY, DEPRESSION,

PARKINSONIAN SYMPTOMS,

BLURRED VISION, DIARRHEA,

INCREASED SALIVATION, CRAMPS,

LACRIMATION, MUSCULAR WEAKNESS,

PARALYSIS, AND FASCICULATION

NEUROTRANSMITTER:
GABA
GAMMA-AMINOBUTYRIC ACID

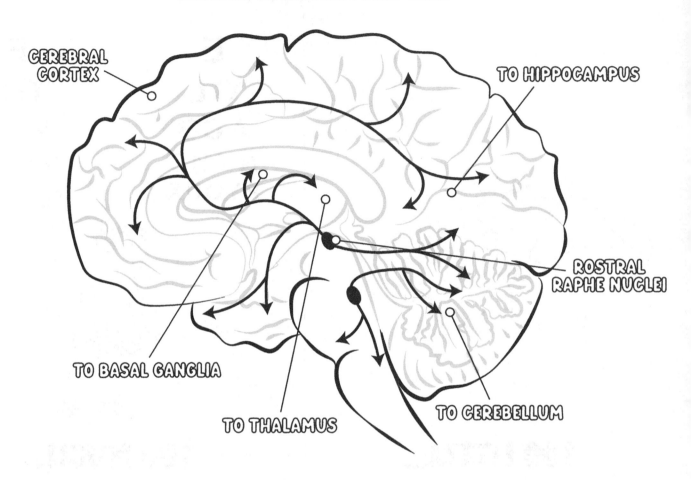

CEREBRAL CORTEX

TO HIPPOCAMPUS

ROSTRAL RAPHE NUCLEI

TO BASAL GANGLIA

TO THALAMUS

TO CEREBELLUM

SYNTHESIZED FROM:
GLUTAMATE

PATHWAYS:
EXPRESSION ACROSS AMYGDALA, HIPPOCAMPUS, HYPOTHALAMUS, PREFRONTAL CORTEX, OLFACTORY BULB, RETINA, AND SPINAL CORD

MAJOR FUNCTIONS OF NEUROTRANSMITTER:
CALMING EFFECT
SLEEP
CONTROLS:
SPINAL REFLEXES
CEREBELLAR REFLEXES
GLYCINE

NEUROTRANSMITTER:
GABA
GAMMA-AMINOBUTYRIC ACID

TOO LITTLE...

RACING THOUGHTS

EPILEPSY

INSOMNIA

ANXIETY

DEPRESSION

SCHIZOPHRENIA

TOO MUCH...

HYPERSOMNIA

REBOUND ANXIETY

NEUROTRANSMITTER:
GLUTAMATE

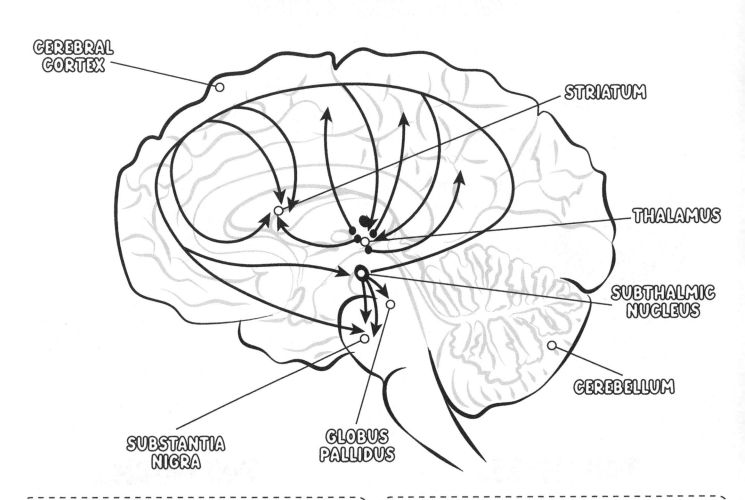

CEREBRAL CORTEX

STRIATUM

THALAMUS

SUBTHALMIC NUCLEUS

CEREBELLUM

SUBSTANTIA NIGRA

GLOBUS PALLIDUS

PRODUCED IN:
SENSORY NEURONS, CEREBRAL CORTEX

PATHWAYS:
CORTICO-CORTICAL PATHWAY...
THE PATHWAYS BETWEEN THE THALAMUS
AND THE CORTEX
EXTRAPYRAMIDAL PATHWAY...
BETWEEN THE CORTEX, SUBSTANTIA NIGRA,
SUBTHALMIC NUCLEUS AND PALLADIUM

MAJOR FUNCTIONS OF NEUROTRANSMITTER:

CREATES LINKS BETWEEN NEURONS

LEARNING

MEMORY

PROCESSING THOUGHTS

SENSORY INPUT

NEUROTRANSMITTER:
GLUTAMATE

TOO LITTLE...

LEARNING AND MEMORY
DIFFICULTIES, DEMENTIA,
NEGATIVE SYMPTOMS
OF SCHIZOPHRENIA:
APATHY, LETHARGY,
WITHDRAWAL FROM SOCIAL
EVENTS OR SETTINGS

TOO MUCH...

OVERSTIMULATION OF THE BRAIN,
RACING THOUGHTS, INSOMNIA,
ANXIETY, EPILEPSY,
PSYCHOSIS
DISEASES: PARKINSON'S,
ALZHEIMER'S, ALS

NEUROTRANSMITTER:
ENDORPHINS

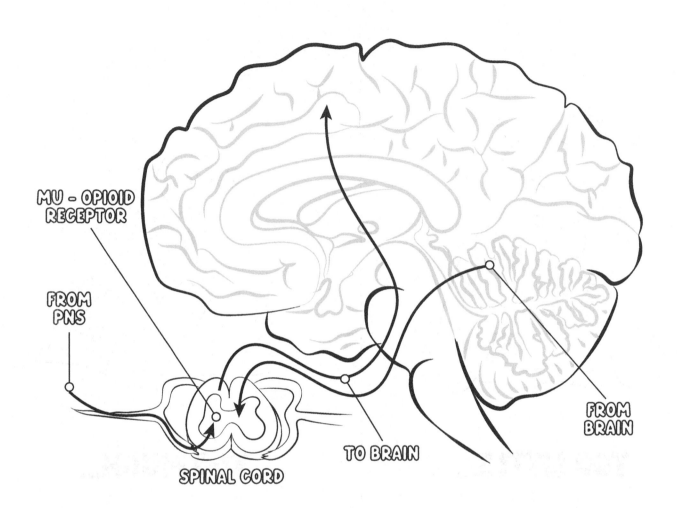

MU - OPIOID RECEPTOR

FROM PNS

FROM BRAIN

TO BRAIN

SPINAL CORD

PRODUCED IN:
PRODUCED AND STORED IN THE PITUITARY GLAND

PATHWAYS:
PERIAQUEDUCTAL GRAY (PAG) AREA

MAJOR FUNCTIONS OF NEUROTRANSMITTER:
NATURAL OPIATE, RELIEVE PAIN, REDUCE STRESS, IMPROVE MOOD, SLOW RESPIRATIONS, PROMPT THE RELEASE OF DOPAMINE

RELEASED THROUGH:
PLEASURABLE ACTIVITIES, PAIN / STRESS

NEUROTRANSMITTER:
ENDORPHINS

TOO LITTLE...

DEPRESSION

ANXIETY

PAIN / BODY ACHES

INSOMNIA

IMPULSIVENESS

ADDICTION

TOO MUCH...

EUPHORIA

RESPIRATORY ARREST

NEUROTRANSMITTER: HISTAMINE

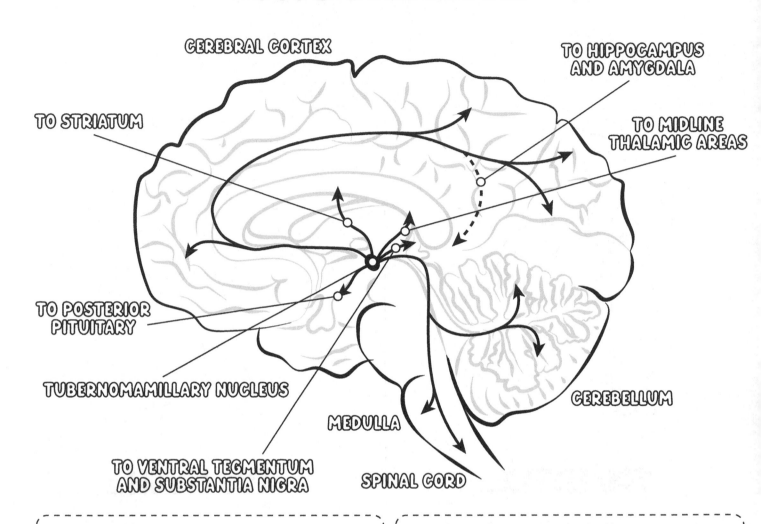

CEREBRAL CORTEX

TO HIPPOCAMPUS AND AMYGDALA

TO STRIATUM

TO MIDLINE THALAMIC AREAS

TO POSTERIOR PITUITARY

TUBERNOMAMILLARY NUCLEUS

CEREBELLUM

MEDULLA

TO VENTRAL TEGMENTUM AND SUBSTANTIA NIGRA

SPINAL CORD

PRODUCED IN:
HYPOTHALAMUS, STOMACH MUCOSA, MAST CELLS, AND BASOPHILS

PATHWAYS:
TUBEROMAMMILLARY NUCLEI OF HYPOTHALAMUS

MAJOR FUNCTIONS OF NEUROTRANSMITTER:

AUTONOMIC & NEUROENDOCRINE REGULATION:

APPETITE

LEARNING & MEMORY

SLEEP REGULATION

MEDIATES INFLAMMATORY REACTION

NEUROTRANSMITTER:
HISTAMINE

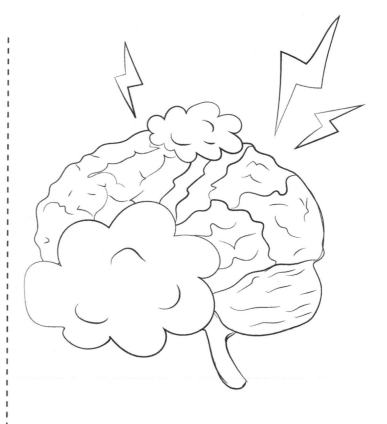

TOO LITTLE...

TOO MUCH...

DEPRESSION

POOR MOTIVATION

HEADACHE

FATIGUE

SLEEP DISTURBANCE

BRAIN FOG

Made in United States
North Haven, CT
20 February 2024

48979061R00033